Bless this mess. This Monday house—
            this cluttered mind—
            this unintentionally haphazard life—
            this confused and confusing world.
We who are housewives do not have the right to sit
down and wallow in the mess we're in.
We have instead an imperative to think with lucidity
            and to act with integrity.
            And this can only be done in prayer.
This book is a collection of prayers—
unorthodox, perhaps,
but the honest outreach of an apprentice.
Lord, bless this mess.

Jo Carr and Imogene Sorley

Bless This Mess
& Other Prayers

Jo Carr and Imogene Sorley

ABINGDON PRESS
NASHVILLE

BLESS THIS MESS

A FESTIVAL BOOK

Published by Jove Publications for Abingdon

Eighteenth Printing 1984
Festival edition published April 1976

ISBN: 0-687-03618-6

Printed in the United States of America

Bless this motley crew

Jim	Cathy
Dougie	Mike
Mark	Glenna
Martha, and	Becky, and
Melissa Sorley	Doug Carr

who have taught us more than several books could tell

Bless This Mess
& Other Prayers

Lord,
  bless this mess.
  Bless this Monday house—
    breakfast dishes in the sink,
    beds still unmade,
    clutter of sandwich makings on the cabinet,
    living room awry.
  Bless this mess,
  and me, as I proceed to tackle it.

Lord,
  bless this mess.
  Bless this Monday mind—
    cluttered and cobwebby,
    catch-all for outgrown opinions and ill-fitting
      prejudices,
    its mental compartments not yet straightened out,
    thought patterns that could do with a good airing.
  Bless this mess
  and me, as I proceed to tackle it.

A Monday house isn't as bad as a Monday mind.
The house can wait.
But there are some *thinking* things that I need to
  attend to now.
I wish it could be done with mop and broom—
those are tools I understand.
But thinking is hard, uncomfortable, unfamiliar.
And thinking is the only cleaning agent for a Monday
  mind.
  Ah, so.

Lord, bless this day.
The mop and broom I can handle. I need thy help with
  the cleansing of my mind.

                    Amen.

O Lord!
That wretched, tousled, mongrel pup
has rooted all my pansies up.
The kids have scattered tinkertoys
from here to breakfast (wretched boys!).
The girls have left their beds unmade.
I feel that I have been betrayed.
Surely I deserve better than this!

Now they've all skittered off to school
and left the mess for me to attend to.
Drat them.

Bless them.
Muddleheaded kids—so like me that sometimes I can't
    stand them.
Made in my own image—that's for sure.
But made as surely, O Lord, in thine.
It is this, it is thee within them,
    to which I am so often blind.
    There is something worthy—eternal—within each
        one of them.

    Help me to see it, shining through.
    Help them see it
    and recognize it
    and know it is of thee.

            Amen.

Lord,
  I don't know much about Mr. Rogers
  (or Mr. Hammerstein, whichever one it was).
But when he wrote about what a beautiful morning,
he must have been absolutely jubilant inside.

And it must have been a day like this one—
  rainwashed,
  diamonds of moisture hanging on the wire fence,
    glistening in the sunlight;
  the smell of tree and sky and joy;
  the uncontainable ecstasy of a mockingbird.
Oh, what a beautiful glorious, azure blue day!

O Lord My God!
When I in awesome wonder
Consider all the worlds thy hands have made, . . .
Then sings my soul, . . .
  *Then sings my soul!**

                    Amen.

* *How Great Thou Art.* Words and music by Stuart K. Hine. © 1955
Manna Music, Inc., Hollywood, California 90028. Used by special permission.

It's kind of hard to think noble thoughts, Lord,
when I just found
three-and-a-half pairs of dirty socks on the bathroom
    floor.

They know better.
Goodness knows I've told them often enough.
    Thoughtless, *care*-less kids.

I make excuses for them.
    They're busy—
        paper routes,
        lots of homework—
        and surely they deserve an occasional unscheduled
            moment.

Still, there are some things they must learn.
And picking up their dirty socks is one of them.

Lord, I need an objective sort of patience.
I need to be able to look at the kids once in a while as
    though they belonged to somebody else.
    To size 'em up—evaluate—
        and stern up my attitude.

I have no call to be mean or gripy or even dogmatic.
But I need to teach them to pick up their socks.

            Amen.

Lord,
may I ask thy blessings on a dull, wooden day?
My reflexes are sluggish,
    my mind foggy,
    my attempts to pray vague and unrewarding.

Why so?
    Shall I blame it on body chemistry?
    Am I coming down with something?
    Or do I still wag around the encumbrance of guilt
        because I chewed out my daughter so acidly last
        night?

No matter.
The day is lumpish,
    but perking up, somehow, just because I'm facing it
    with thee.

How impoverished we would be if we could come to thee
    only in those exulting moments of joy.
How lonely, if we could find thee only when the day
    was a shining one.
You know the kind of odd-body I am, Lord—
    joyful today and glum tomorrow.
    Glad—mad—dull—devious—
    thrilled to the shoelaces or just plain blah.

I thank you that life is so.
How stagnating to feel always the same.
Thank you for the kaleidoscope of living.
Thank you for this dull, wooden, thou-art-here-also day!

                    Amen.

He had had it. Too much pressure.
Too many trying experiences in a new situation.
Starting junior high *can* be traumatic.
An assignment forgotten.
And an F math paper that he had to get signed.
He has small shoulders, Lord. I should have seen that
    all this was simply more than they could carry.
But seeing, I perceived not.
I felt pressured. And put upon.
Ashamed that *my* child made an F.
Accusing.

I'm sorry, Lord. What he needed was not added weight
    to his burden,
  but an arm around the shoulder,
  a cup of hot chocolate,
  a run around the block together.
  A lift. A boost.
  Maybe even a confession—for I was his age once
    and forgot things—
    and made an F.

Lord, give me the . . . what?
    The maturity?
    The emotional balance?
    The wisdom and love.
Let me, seeing, perceive.

            Amen.

Why me, Lord?
Here I am.
"In the thick of things."

Once I wasn't.
Someday I won't be.
But here, now, I am.
Right in the middle of a strange, mixed-up world.
And with this nagging awareness within me
    that you want *me*
        to *do* something
        or *say* something
        or *be* something
    that shall make a difference.

It may not change the course of history—
    this that you want me to say or do or be—
but it may change the course of some life.
    Mine?
    His?
    Hers?
    Theirs?
And I am obligated to respond to thy call
    on behalf of all mankind.
Why me, Lord?
I don't know why. I only know the unrest, the divine
discontent, the eagerness on one hand to charge off in
knightly splendor
    in service for thee,
and the agony on the other of not knowing in what direction.

Why me, Lord?
And what, *what* would you have me do?

          Amen.

It takes *courage*
   to be crocus-minded.

Lord, I'd rather wait until June,
   like wise roses,
   when the hazards of winter are safely behind,
      and I'm expected,
      and everything's ready for roses.

But crocuses?
   Highly irregular.
   Knifing up through hard-frozen ground and snow,
      sticking their necks out.
   because they *believe* in spring
   and have something personal
      and emphatic to say about it.

Lord, I am by nature rose-minded.
   Even when I have studied the situation here
   and know there are wrongs that need righting,
   affirmations that need stating,
   and know also that my speaking out may offend—
      for it rocks the boat—
   well, I'd rather wait until June.
   Maybe later things will work themselves out,
   and we won't have to make an issue of it.

Lord, forgive.
   Wrongs don't work themselves out.
   Injustices and inequities and hurt don't just dissolve.

Somebody has to stick his neck out,
   somebody who cares enough
      to think through
      and work through hard ground,
   because he believes
   and has something personal
      and emphatic to say about it.

Me, Lord?
   Crocus-minded?

Could it be that there are things that need to be said, and you want me to say them?

I pray for courage.

Amen.

Lord,
I got to thinking about Amos.
Two thousand, three thousand years ago, he knew the
stars, the same stars we know, and called them by name.

> He who made Pleiades and Orion,
>> and turns deep darkness into the morning,
>> and darkens the day into night
> who calls for the waters of the sea,
>> and pours them out upon the surface of the
>> earth,
> the Lord is his name!

Thy universe, Lord, is so vast,
  so incomprehensible.
I cannot think in light years.
I cannot think big enough to understand the magnitude
  of space.
I even have trouble thinking of Amos
  so many years ago,
  struggling with this same vast heaven of stars
  and calling them by name,
  and knowing *even then* that they all were part of thy
    creation,
    even as he was a part,
    even as I am a part.
Lord, God, Creator of Orion and Pleiades and all the
  universe,
    who set planets in orbit,
    who arranged the galaxies in their order,
      and who made me a living soul,
    holy is thy name.

Amen.

My problem, Lord,
is that I'm insecure.
I need a blanket, like Linus.
Or an apron string.
   I wish Mama were here to make the decisions.
   She'd see that things were attended to.

Come to think of it, childhood was a pretty good racket—
   somebody else around to tell me what to do,
      when to do it,
      and usually how.
      No decisions.
      The rules all clear cut and readable.
      No sweat.
      That's security.
But, then, what's so secure about me—grown up, and
still unwilling to make my own decisions?
Childhood is a real good deal—
   for children.
But not for me.

      When I was a child,
      I spoke like a child,
      I thought like a child,
      I reasoned like a child;
      When I became a man, I gave up childish ways.

My "apron strings" were severed a long time ago.
It's high time I gave up my immature, impotent, child-
ish ways.

      Amen.

Meditation on Decorating the Christmas Tree*

Good grief! I'm getting swamped again.
The month of dither? Amen, amen!
Gotta get a costume made for Kay
To be in that dratted Christmas play.
(She's the angel with the missing teeth.)
Still haven't made the Christmas wreath.
Still haven't chosen a gift for John.
(Why won't this string of lights turn on?)
Open house at the Browns' tonight.
(Why won't this ornament dangle right?)
Is *this* the day I promised Ben
I'd take him down to the five and ten?
I'll lose my mind while he makes up his;
Before he's through, I'll be in a tizz.
(Now what shall I put right over there?
That part of the tree looks a little bare.)
I'm due at school at a quarter to three
To help the Scouts take a Christmas tree
Down to the Mission, and when they're through,
I've gotta stop back at the school for Sue;
And *what* can I fix for supper tonight?
Goodness! The living room looks a fright—
But there! The tree is a lovely thing.
And the angel on top with hovering wing
Is smiling down as she has these years
(I could see her better, except for the tears).
Forgive my dither! Nor let me fret,
Nor let me, Lord, so soon forget
How I love Sue, and Ben, and Kay,
And John—and thee—and Christmas Day.
Forgive my dither, Lord, I pray.

Amen.

* Reprinted by permission from *Christian Home*, December, 1966. Copyright © 1966 by Graded Press.

Lord,
    I'm tired.
    The burdens that are mine to carry are heavy indeed.
        And constant.
        And depressing.
        Uummhh.
    They may seem small to someone else, but someone
    else isn't carrying them.

I'm sorry, Lord.
I guess I'm just burden-conscious today.
My burden conscious.

Some problems can be battled,
others can only be borne.
And they get heavy.
They get in the way of living.
Sometimes I get so tangled up in my problems that I let
whole days go by—unnoticed,
                        unenjoyed,
                        unlived,
    because I *am* burden conscious.
But the sun still shines;
    the daffodils outside my window are incomparably
    yellow.
In my better moments I know that thou art with me.
That being so,
    the burden is not mine alone.
Thank you, Lord.

                Amen.

Dear Lord,
burnt sienna—
   and azure blue!
For surety I know why,
for brown is the color of earth and soil,
and blue is the shade of the sky.
And here in between, with my feet on the ground and
my heart in the heavens, am I.

It must be "both-and," Lord.
You haven't called me to some vague, absent-minded
saintliness,
   wherein I read spiritual classics
   while my children run unattended.
Neither have you called me to spend my every waking
moment
   scrubbing floors and serving church suppers
   and filling baskets for The Needy
   while my soul goes unattended.

Burnt sienna—earthen hue.
   Keep me practical, Lord,
   aware of the place that floor wax and baking powder
      have in my daily way of life.
Azure blue—heavenly hue.
   Let my soul sing—
      while I'm polishing floors and baking our daily
      bread.

Amen.

Lord,
    she *priested* to me.
    It had been so long since I had seen her,
    and I began to babble about the kids
        and how busy we all are
        and how she "hadn't changed a bit"—
        saying nothing.
    Then she looked at me—
    caught and held me with her eyes—
    wanting to know how it goes with me,
    wanting to know what my hopes and hurts and needs
    really are, caring—
    willing to bear with me the burdens that are mine
        or share with me the joys.
    Surface chit-chat seemed suddenly out of place.
    And we talked, in depth.

    I would have let the moment go by,
        but she *priested* to me.
    And the time we had together became significant.
    I am afraid to speak, so, to those I meet,
        afraid I might be misunderstood,
        afraid I might be intruding.
    She did not intrude.
    She cared enough to risk offending me, to risk re-
        jection.
    She cared enough to reach within.
    And, in doing so, she *priested* to me.
Lord, I rush in babbling.
Let me pause
    and perceive
    and risk
    and love enough to speak.

                    Amen.

"From ghoulies and ghosties and long-leggety beasties
And things that go bump in the night,
  Good Lord, deliver us!"

Sounds quaint, Lord. And old. And not for me.
The goblins that scared grandpa seem pretty toothless
today.
He didn't have to worry about A-bombs or H-bombs
  or worse-yet-to-come bombs.
His ghosties were drought or flood
                        and no beans in the pantry,
                        doubt or death
                        and no faith to lean on.
Come to think of it, my ghosties are about the same.
I'm afraid of
  not being able to pay the bills,
  of the kind of world this is becoming,
  of wars, hot and cold, near and far,
  of riots and rebellions,
  of being unable to measure up when it is vitally
    important that I do so,
  of facing things I can't cope with.
These are the ghosties that go "bump" in my night—
these and other vague, unsettling, nameless fears.
Good Lord, deliver us.
Me. Deliver *me* from fear.
In thee do I put my trust.

                        Amen.

Father, forgive.
That devotion I had to lead, for circle meeting—
you know. I got the words out of a book.
They were good words, and I said them right well,
I thought.
I could see the other women were impressed, too.
They looked at me—well, gratefully—
as though I had found that for which they hunger.
And I had not.
Their praise was warmly given,
but it brought no warmth to me,
for I was counterfeit.
The words were not mine. They had merely come
from a book.

Father, forgive.
Forgive me for holding before my face a mask of
saintliness, to hide the poverty of my own soul.
Forgive my withholding.
I keep nibbling at the edges of the Eternal.
I respond to that divine magnetism which draws me toward thee,
and then I balk, unwilling to experience for myself
that which the book says can be.

Father, forgive.
I really do want to be real, to be whole.
Forgive my unwillingness.
And minister to my fears.

Amen.

Lord, I believe . . . .
>I think.
Why this uncertainty, Lord?
Why these nagging doubts?
I am convinced that this whole vast and unbelievable
universe is thy creation.
It didn't just happen.
I didn't just happen.
>As surely as you made the stars in the sky and the
earth and the sun and the moon—you made me.
>While you were at it, you planted within me a lone-
liness for thee.
All this I believe;
>all this I *know*.

So why, Lord, these nagging doubts?
Why these withholdings?
Why this unwillingness to trust thee all the way?

Part of it, I know, is my reluctance to let someone else—
even you, Lord—tell me what to do.
Like an unruly child, I am vaguely aware that you
know what is best for me, would always do what is best
for me.
But I, stubbornly, unruly child that I am,
>want to
>>go my own way,
>>make my own mistakes,
>>rule my own life.
And for this I pay the price of estrangement.
Lord, I believe.
Help thou my unbelief.

Amen.

Good grief, Lord!

Surveyor, with its spindly legs, sits on the surface of the
moon, taking pictures of the craters and plains around
it.

The "93 elements which are the entire chemical
make-up of the universe" have become 103, and
scientists are looking for others. There's no top limit
on knowledge anymore.

DNA, RNA—biochemistry stands on the brink of creating the controlled personality.

Knowledge is compounding itself.

And I'm all shook up.

I'm a little scared, sometimes. Maybe we are meddling
in divine affairs.

Not so. You gave us minds, Lord.

You meant us to use them in the search for truth.

And wherever this search shall lead us, you are already
there.

There is no truth that is not of thee.

While man was learning to strike spark from flint and
steel, you know that atoms split and fuse.

From the beginning you have known the truths that the
keenest human minds now only dimly perceive.

What breathtaking discoveries lie ahead of us?

Lord, God of truth,
    who can see our bumbling pursuit after little truths,
what a jubilance that I am allowed to be a part of life
at a time like this.

What a wondrous, jubilant day to be alive!

Amen.

Dear Lord,

I am concerned—genuinely concerned—about the affairs of the universe.

I've pondered the problems of political ideology, of poverty, of war, of population explosion, and of civil rights.

Big problems.

They challenge because they are big problems. They call for mass action, herculean efforts. And I'm eager to plunge in. To save the world.

So what do I *do*, Lord?

How can I help slay these dragons?

I've already studied the problem,
> formed a committee,
> held discussions,
> made speeches.

And the problems are still there, bigger than ever. Why can't I get my teeth into the big problems?

You know, Lord,

I keep looking for the grand and glorious chance to serve

> and miss the everyday opportunities that are staring me in the face.

I ponder the problems of international relationships but have not contributed anything creative to my own relationship with my next-door neighbor.

Poverty? There's a spine-tingling excitement about worldwide statistics. But *real* poverty, down on the other end of *my* street, is dirt and squalor—a depressing thing that I want no part of.

I begin to see.

You're not calling me to be honorary chairman of the International Committee for the Mentally Retarded, but you may be asking me to help with a Sunday school class for the retarded children in my own community.

You aren't asking for dramatic effort for noble causes, but for dogged perserverance on the here-where-I-am tasks.

Big challenges are easy to see—maybe because they
 are comfortably vague and far off.
It takes insight and intestinal fortitude to sweat out the
 little challenges.

I'm rather short on insight
 and intestinal fortitude.
Sharpen my sword, Lord. I've got some everyday-type
 dragons to slay.

Amen.

Bless the Lord, O my soul,
  and all that is within me
  bless his holy name.

All the love that is within me
    and the intellect
    and these small talents which I possess—
    let them bless his holy name.
  And let the untapped resources within me,
      which I have not yet even thought of,
      bless his holy name.

Bless the Lord, O my soul,
  and forget not all his benefits.
  For he has given me hands
      that can sew a jumper, or paint a garage, or write
      a letter,
      eyes that can see a burnished oak leaf, or a tear,
      ears that can catch the wonder of symphony, of
      sermon, of a childish chuckle.
  For he has given me a heart full of gladness, a cup
    running over.

Bless the Lord, O my soul.

                    Amen.

Well, Lord,
    this is really a mess of things.
    Just look at the fix we're in.
All because of this ridiculous experiment of making us
        free to choose—
    free to fight, and gripe, and rebel,
    free to get our kicks from bottles, or pills, or a
        hypodermic needle,
    free to be slobs or blobs.

You could have *made* us worthy.
    It sure would have been easier.
    It seems I've got to go this Christian route,
        but it would be simpler if it were automatic.

It's not that I mind doing right.
It's the daily frustration of deciding what *is* right,
    of having to choose between two "rights,"
    of having to choose
    and decide
    and be responsible for what I decide.

You could have made me . . . a puppet?
God, forbid.
I don't want to be anybody's puppet. Even yours.
    I want to be free.
    I want to be *me*.
Thank you, Lord, for the gift of integrity.
Without the freedom to blunder and stumble,
    I have not the power to become.

Help me *become* worthy.

                    Amen.

We few, we happy few, we band of brothers. . . .

That's how it is, Lord,
　exultant, somehow,
　　　to see her move into the new interracial crisis in
　　　　her block, lovingly—
　　　to see him face up to personal disaster, nobly—
　　　to see them accept the hard challenge of the new
　　　　role their church must play, sacrificially.
　And I exult in this thy fellowship!

This is a conspiracy of the concerned—
　each involved because of his own dedication to thee,
　each committed to a common trust on behalf of all
　　mankind,
　and each rejoicing in the strength of the others,
　exulting in their jubilance,
　deeply moved by their commitment.

I thank thee, Lord, for this fellowship of believers.

Amen.

Lord,
    things are as they are.
    My richly embroidered daydreams do not alter them
    any.
    Some things just are.

So . . .
now what?
Do I spend the next thirty years
    or the next thirty days
    or even the next thirty minutes
blubbering about it?

I could, Lord. You'd listen.
But it wouldn't change things.
Except me.
    It would diminish me.
    It would leave me spent. And frustrated.
        And less than I was meant to be.
Better I should use my next thirty years—
yes, and my next thirty minutes—
working with the situation,
    as it is.
Better I should look it square in the face
    and accept it
and then pick life up and start from here.
    God, give the serenity to accept those things which
        cannot be changed.

                Amen.

Lord,
    it's only me,
pursuing something I'm not sure of.

    It's only me,
looking for a road map. Or a set of rules.

I like things clear cut and specific, Lord.
And when you ask me to accept "on faith," you ask a
    hard thing.
What *is* faith, anyway,
    but committing myself to something I'm not sure of?

All of which is further complicated, Lord, when I find
    out how many of the things that I *am* sure of aren't
    so. I thought this table was solid. Now I hear that
    "matter is basically nonmaterial"—mostly empty
    space between cells.
I was sure of a friend—and found her feet were clay.
I am sure of me—and found myself less than my
    image.

And you, Lord,
    of whom I have been so sure—and so agonizingly
    unsure—you emerge as the only absolute.
I pray for solid certainty.
But I'll settle, Lord, for this growing awareness,
and count myself rich indeed.

                    Amen, amen.

I can talk to *her*, Lord,
   because with me she wears no mask.
   So I don't have to wear my mask either.
   I can be me—just plain, unvarnished me—
   and this transparency makes it possible to communi-
   cate.

Why is it so rarely so?
Most of the time I cling tenaciously to the security
   of a mask—
   hiding behind social amenities,
   covering up my fear of inadequacy with pointless
   chit-chat,
   filling my days with organized busyness,
   hiding behind my socially acceptable mask.
      Which isn't me.
      Which isn't worthy.
      Which doesn't communicate with anyone.

I'll not change overnight, Lord,
   but I shall meet someone else this day.
   Give me the courage to loose my mask.
Let me be quiet for a moment, listen with a third ear,
   listen to that which longs to be said.
   For if I wear no mask with her, perhaps she may
   feel free to wear none with me;
      and we can communicate.
And oh, the relief,
      the release,
in accepting, and being accepted, with honesty—
the inexpressible comfort of feeling safe with a
person.

                    Amen.

Lord, I wish I could yodel!
I just don't see how any other mortal sound can express
   my joy.

   No excuse, really.
No bonanza.
Just the glorious gift of this day,
   my day,
      and thine.
     Joy doesn't need an excuse. It just needs to yodel.

I thank thee, Lord,
   that I am alive this day.
   Not just "undead,"
     but *alive,*
        seeing the sycamore balls dangling from the
          trees, as they have dangled, unseen, all fall;
        hearing the crunch of snow;
        exulting, delighting, glorying in this yodeling
          sort of day.
I thank thee, Lord.

            Amen.

Lord,
   how is it that when I lift my eyes to thee
so often all I see is that splat of oatmeal on the kitchen
ceiling and a new crack in the paint?

I want to do glorious deeds—
   but I have to iron white shirts
   and bake cupcakes for the Brownie meeting.
I want to be a saint—one of the architects of the king-
      dom—
   but you know, better than I do,
   that I'm considerably less than a saint.

And yet somehow the most honest meditation I have
   known has happened over an ironing board.
   A most honest sort of love can be stirred into a batch
      of cupcakes.

I don't really have to see visions
to be aware of thy nearness.
I don't really have to achieve saintliness
to know thy love.

Thank you, Lord.
Thank you for not requiring of me
   that which I cannot do
                           or see
                           or be.

Help me worship, and serve, and love
in the ways that I know.

                    Amen.

I care. I have feelings.
But I hide them.
It isn't that I am *ashamed* of caring.
It's just that people are not supposed to show their
emotions.

I am not sure why.
Folks used to. Like the old-timey letters that told of
yearning, of loving, of the way they *really* felt about
each other.
I write about the weather—and the boys robbing the
bees—and make it a conversation piece.
Paul could have done that.
He could have said, "Hope things are going real fine
for you Philippians."
But he didn't.
He wrote from the heart: "I thank my God upon
every remembrance of you."
It was a real letter of love, and said so.

We get along these days without disclosing how we
feel—
without using expressions of endearment,
without shedding tears of grief, or of relief,
or of joy—
without the touch of a hand,
the blessed reaching out of the heart when
words are not enough.
We *can* keep our emotions under tight control.

But what spice it adds to life,
what meaning it adds to lives,
when we let our hearts show!

Grant me the maturity to show my love.

Amen.

Lord, I've had it.
   Up to here.
A crisis I can cope with.
But the everlasting picayune frustrations
   are driving me out of my mind.

A crisis I could grapple with.
   If I lost my leg, I think I could adjust—with some
      nobility, too.
   But what's noble about a corn on my little toe?
   What's challenging about a cold that hangs on and
   on and on?

The faucet drips, Lord.
That kid forgot his books again.
It is impossible to get everything clean at once because,
   while I am ironing, the wash piles up.
I've had it—and had it.

I wish you had called me to a grand task,
   a clear-cut and noble endeavor,
   instead of the frustrations of my every day.
   Which is what I am called to—
      called to pray while the faucet drips,
      called to priest to my neighbor while my corn
         hurts,
      called to fix faucets
      and to maintain the sense of humor that realizes
         I am not all that far behind on my ironing—
         I'm just *ahead* on my washing!
It is a matter of perspective.
In perspective, frustrations *are* little things.
   I can cope.

                    Amen.

Dear Lord, I come confessing.
   To live dangerously in these days is unavoidable.
   But to live ignorantly is inexcusable.
      And I live ignorantly.

      I voted today.
      Civic duty, and all that.
      But for the most part I voted ignorantly.
      I just didn't bother to study the issues.
      And those issues will affect me, affect all of us.

   I don't plan my days. They just come.
   I don't plan my tomorrows either.
      Mine is a "live one day at a time" casualness that
      constitutes living ignorantly.

And I guess it *is* inexcusable
   to spend more real thought on choosing a dress
      pattern than on the Eternals.

Lord, God,
   I would live intentionally.
   Thought-fully.
   Not by default.
      but by design.

                    Amen.

Lord,
  status quos are safe.
  My problems are old, familiar, comfortable, status-
  quo problems.
  Why should I swap them for unknown and maybe
  bigger ones?

And yet, I am not content with a "comfortable," sta-
tus-quo life.
  There is within me this restlessness,
  this fleeting, recurring, nagging awareness
  that Life should be something tremendous,
    whereas *my* life is mostly trivial.
And I am again confronted with the Way.
Do I have to stick my neck out?
  Isn't there some other way?

I stuck my neck out when I married.
  I knew there would be risks—unknown—a price.
  But I was willing to accept the risks along with the
  rewards. And I've been deeply glad.
We stuck our necks out when we decided to have a
child.
  We knew there would be problems, heartaches, un-
    foreseeable "costs."
  But we were willing, eager to invest ourselves in a
  family.
  And we are deeply glad.
Now this.
  You ask me to accept abundant life.
  All I have to do is surrender my will to thine.
But I'm afraid of the unforeseeable costs.
Ah, Lord, it's like all the rest of life. What I really
want, I am willing to pay the price for.
  I really want thee.

          Amen.

Lord,
the folks down the street have put their house up for
sale because a family whose skin is "not like ours" has
moved into their block.

That's no Christian attitude, Lord,
and it makes me seethe to see thy children feel
bitterly toward others,
who are also thy children.

But, Lord, the fact is, I too have a blind spot.
I'm really not sure how I'll feel when it happens in my
block.
For even now I know a strain, when I talk to a "different" one.
I call it a "language barrier"—
or excuse it as "different backgrounds, you know."
But it's there, and it is an impediment to friendship.
It is an unworthy attitude.
It is unchristian, Lord, and it is an impediment to the
growth of the Kingdom.

Each heritage is a noble one.
Each contributes so richly to what we all are.
The Negro's sense of rhythm, which moves and
sways and sings within him;
the Oriental's sense of beauty in small things—
a spray of apple blossoms, or of pine—
a few delicate strokes of a watercolor brush;
the Latin's sense of pleasure in today—
enjoyment of children, of music, of his own culture;
the Anglo's orderliness, which enables him to get
things done.

All are noble heritages, Lord.
All are part of thy divine scheme of things.
Let me see, Lord. Let me see through the color of
skin—
to be no more conscious of that than I am of color
of hair—
see through to the real person within, who also
dreams dreams, and has hopes, and prays prayers.
I covet this discernment.

Amen.

> A man don't mind if the stars grow dim
> Or the clouds blow over and darken him
> As long as the Lord God's watchin' over them
> Keeping track how it all goes on.*

The Lord God—
    Creator of all that is, or ever was, or ever shall be—
    is keeping watch.

Keeping watch over me
    and mine.
    Over nations and peoples—
    willful beings, all.
Like children.
    Straying, trying, stumbling—
    learning a little somehow—
    engrossed in their own terribly
      important piddling.

Keeping watch.
    Not interfering,
    not manipulating,
but aware of his own divine plan.
    Calling,
    challenging,
    daring us to be better,
and keeping track how it all goes on.

Lord God—
let me respond, lucidly,
to that part of thy divine plan
which is *my* responsibility.

Amen.

Dear Lord,
   help me teach my child the worth of the men who
sweep our streets
and grade our country roads.
   There are so many whose names I don't know—
   whose faces I don't even know—
   who, by performing their daily tasks,
   make it possible for me to perform mine.
      I have only to empty the trash.
      If I had to haul it to the city dump, well,
         it would cut a hunk out of my day.
         I wouldn't even do it until I had to.
         And neither would my neighbors.
      We have only to shovel the snow off our own
      drive.
         But we ride to work and school and the grocery
            store on streets already cleared for us during
            the night.
      Ad infinitum.
Help me remember my debt to them.
Help me remember to mention this debt to my children,
   reminding them of the worthiness of labor,
   of the worth of any task performed for the common
   good.
Help me to undertake my own daily tasks as for the
common good.
Help me teach my children that they too have a life-
long responsibility—
   for the common good.

                    Amen.

Fools rush in, Lord.
I do.
Barging, bumblefooted and blind, into a delicate
  moment.

She stood on tiptoe to look into the rose,
deep into its very center. I don't know what
secrets she saw there
or what worlds of wonder.
But it was no time to call her to make her bed.
Nor was it a time to rush out and deliver an in-
  formative lecture on botany.
It was a moment for *not* interfering.
  I usually do, for bumblefootedness and blindness
  are among my "little sins."
I get so preoccupied with the things I think they ought
  to be doing that I forget to leave them alone with the
  wonders of the universe.

There are times when the progress of an inchworm
  is of more profound significance than the dust on the
  piano.

And there are times when aloneness is good for the
  soul,
    when solitude—so hard to come by for a child—
    is a redeeming thing
    and should not be intruded upon.
I remember such moments, Lord, from my own child-
time.

Creative restraint—
    I need it, to insure for my own children
    such moments of discovery and wonder.

Amen.

Lord, I have been befriended.

It was not easy.
I have a nice, warm feeling toward those whom I
have chosen to befriend.
But sometimes I have been unwilling to accept a
relationship which asks more than surface amenities—
embarrassed at proffered friendship,
unwilling to open up,
unwilling to be "beholden,"
aware of "debt,"
but longing, even so, for a deep rapport with a
kindred spirit.
And she befriended me.
Sensing my reticence, and my withholding,
sensing, too, my need,
she brought me a rose.
She happened by to visit one day.
She took my kids to the park when I was sick.
She touched my hand.
With the gentle persistence of one who cares she
has become a part of my life—
and I have been befriended.

Lord, it is even so with you.
You have befriended me over my protests,
in spite of my withholdings—when I was
unwilling to accept a relationship that asked more
than surface amenities,
unwilling to open up,
unwilling to become "beholden,"
but longing, even so, for a deep rapport with the
universe.

And I have been befriended.

Amen, amen.

Dear Lord,
forgive.
I have been gnawing-and-nagging again.
  Discipline they need—
    objective, appropriate discipline.
  But they don't need to leave the house in the morning
    with words of reproach heavy around them, or
    with the mental picture of my furrowed brow and
    tight pinched lips.
  Discipline is necessary and character building.
  Gnawing-and-nagging is destructive.

  Besides, it gives me wrinkles.
  And headaches.
  And ulcers.
  It gives me a blight-scarred appreciation of my
    kids, who lose individuality under by merciless
    yammering, and become merely my scapegoats.
  It gives me an eroded image of myself.
So, Lord,
  I'd best rethink things.
  I need to *see* my children—realize that they need
    my shown love,
    my spoken encouragement,
    my valid help,
    as genuinely as they need correction.
This is the only chance I have to guide them. Let me
not flub it,
    nor decry my love for them
    with hasty, thoughtless gnawing and nagging.

                    Amen.

Lord, God,
    you have not called me
        to some puttering, petty, mundane mediocrity.

You have called me to renew the world.
    This is my task.
    Impossible?
    Unreachable?
        Imperative.

Not all at once.
Not by revolution, at least not the blood-and-thunder
    kind.
But by revolution in the hearts of people.
    Starting with me.

You have called me to renew the world—
    at coffee klatsch,
    at supper table,
    in circle meeting,
    at the polls,
    in a letter to the editor,
    in a letter to a friend.

These are merely puttering, petty, mundane things, un-
less they are done with all my mind
                        and strength
                        and soul
                        and heart . . .
                            and done for thee.

To renew the world—
this is my task.
God, help me.

                    Amen.

Lord, it's like second wind.
Athletes get it
    when they have spent themselves.

When they have spent themselves.
Totally committed to the race or the game,
    they give all they've got.
And then (from whence?) this second wind—this new
    burst of life and vitality.

Could it be . . .
    when we have *spent* ourselves
        in search for thee—
    totally committed to the quest, pushing beyond
        first layers of fatigue—
        we tap a new level of energy
        which we have not known before,
        which has not been ours because we have not
            pushed far enough to find it?

Second wind.
And it carries us
    farther than . . .
    closer than . . .
        beyond placid piety,
        to finding the Supreme Context in which we
            rightfully belong.
Second wind.

I press on toward the high calling.

                    Amen.

Lord, the preacher said we ought to pray for humility.

Why?

You don't really want me to grovel.
It isn't worms you need to establish the Kingdom.
It isn't miserable wretches wallowing in their self-abasement.

What *is* humility, anyway?
Maybe it's got nothing to do with self-abasement.
Is it—not so much dwelling on my own weakness
   as acknowledging that you are the source of my
   strength?

Lord of life,
   who am I that thou art mindful of me?
   Just an ordinary mortal.
   But I have been given a mind
                         and strength
                         and the power of becoming.
I have been called to the utterly glorious possibilities of
   sonship.

So—I walk tall,
   taking responsibility for my failures,
   and glorying in thy strength.
      I thank thee, Lord.
                  Amen.

Lord,
I keep thinking about Brother Lawrence,
  who *practiced* the presence of God,
    even as he went about his duties in the gloomy old
    monastery kitchen.
And I wonder, sometimes, if it might have been easier
  then.

I'll bet Brother Lawrence didn't have to struggle with
  the knob on the washer that has stripped its gears,
  nor with a mule-headed old car.
The monks might have tracked mud into the monastic
  dining hall,
    but Brother Lawrence used a simple and
    uncomplicated mop to cope with it.

What Brother Lawrence had was simplicity—
  of life and of purpose.
What I've got is multiplicity—
  of life and of purpose.
  Must it be thus, Lord?
Gadgets are meant to be labor-*saving* devices.
They should free me for more important things, not
  overwhelm my days.

Maybe *his* secret was more than merely simplicity.
Not all uncomplicated lives are saintly.
Maybe his secret was that he *practiced*
  thy presence—
    sought thee out, deliberately,
                        daily,
                        devotedly
                        this above all else,
until he was able to live life
                        in thy presence.

                Amen.

Ah, Lord,
    the little ways in which we trade away our lives!

Forgive.
Forgive the stupidity that allows us to demean our sonship
    by cheating
    or gossiping,
    by withholding forgiveness,
    by magnifying the thoughtlessness of another until it
        becomes a wall,
    by frittering away our irretrievable days.

When we stoop to belittle,
when we enjoy an off-color joke,
when we compromise,
    we give away part of our worth.
    We are less.

And for such *little* things, Lord.

Like the nightingale who sold his feathers
    (one by surely-I-won't-miss-just-one)
    for a bucket of worms,
    we sell our ability to reach the unreachable sky for
        such unworthy little things.

Father, forgive.

    Help us remember
        that we are children of the Almighty God.

        Amen.*

* A shorter version of this selection originally appeared in *The Christian Home*, January, 1969. Copyright © 1968, Graded Press.

Lord, thy mockingbird fills the new morning
with a song of uninhibited joy!
  Later today he will hunt berries and seed.
  Later today he will drive the sparrows from his
    domain
  and perhaps tease the cat.

But for this moment he is completely consumed with
  joy.

I thank thee, Lord, for such moments.
Thy creatures express it—
  a lamb, gamboling in spring grass;
  a pup, uninhibited, uncoordinated, and utterly
    jubilant;
  a child, exulting in new shoes
      or bare feet
      or hot cookies.
I thank thee for the privilege of seeing their moments.

And I thank thee from the very depths of my being
when such moments come to me,
and I too know uncontainable joy.
Like now.
Standing here, in the clear cold of early morn,
  seeing that star—is it Venus?—
  shining in the east,
  with all the added brilliance of not-quite-dawn.
Standing here alone—with thee—
  calling the children to come and see.

Later this day I shall mop and dust my small domain
  and feed the cat.
But for this moment I am completely consumed with
  joy.
  I thank thee, Lord.

          Hallelujah!

So blind.
So blind am I, in thy all-seeing gaze,
    thinking only this path on which I try to walk leads
    to thee.
    Thinking only these formulas which I try to use,
                only these prayers, framed in my own
                    terms,
                only these good deeds and acceptable
                    services.
                can reach thee.
So blind am I.

Lord, there is no single road—
                no guaranteed formula.
Do I fail to reach thee *because* of my striving?
For that by its very nature bespeaks a *self*-conscious-
ness, a feeling of I-do-this-to-win-my-crown.

Can it be that I shall find thee, when I do not so much
    seek *thee,* as seek *thine;*
    when I do not consciously give *a* gift,
                        a deed,
                        a thing,
    but become lost in a task, totally involved in life;
    when I shall not so much *give,*
    as simply not withhold, any part of self?

So blind am I,
too earth-spawned and self-oriented to see.

I pray for clarity, Lord,
    for vision.

                    Amen.

Lord, it's the principle of the thing.
I am being put-upon—
    asked to change my neat and orderly plans,
    asked to make more-than-my-share concessions,
    for the good of the cause.
I don't like to have my plans messed up.
Even for good causes.
Even for worthy needs.
Even for thee, Lord.

I'm not called to make concessions often.
What I *ought* to do
    is usually what I wanted to do anyway,
    and it's easy to slip into the attitude that this is
        enough.
Then, when something comes along,
    as it just has,
    and I am required to make my concession,
    it looms before me as a Great Sacrifice.

Instead of undertaking
    joyfully,
    gratefully,
    because of the opportunity to participate in thy will,
        I rebel
        and complain
        and drag my feet.
What *is* important—
    my neat and orderly little plans
    or thy divine scheme of things?

If all of me were committed to thee,
    I guess I wouldn't even have a problem.
    I'm sorry, Lord.

              Amen.

O Lord, forgive our pigheaded bigotry.
  It was a church paper basically, and it said,
  "We have all the answers,
    and we know they work."

Answers?
We don't even know all the questions!
And what poverty of the soul is ours
  when we think we understand thee, all-in-all,
  when we think our finite minds
    can comprehend the Almighty God!

"And we know they work"?
  Faith by formula.
  Guaranteed godliness.
O Lord, forgive our pigheaded bigotry.

All I know—all I need to know—
is that I am thine,
that I am loved,
and that I am called.

I can worship only in spirit and in truth,
  following that call wherever it leads,
  without having to know all the answers.

This is not blindness, but clarity—
          a clarity of identity,
           of knowing who I am
            and whose I am.
It brings a disturbance, needling me to action.
And it brings a peace, which is not placidity
  but exhilaration.
O thou incomprehensible Father of life. . . .

       Amen.

Lord,
  the children talk about "the olden days,"
  when I was young—
  that inconceivable long ago when TV was not,
    and the drip pan under the icebox ran over,
    and cars were all black and the horns went
    "oooogah."

And I grin—exulting a little within to have been
  a part of it all,
  to have witnessed so much change.
Let me never begrudge the encroaching years!
They will bring changes too—
  changes that stagger the imagining.
  And this too I shall be allowed to witness.

My years have spanned the crossover between two
eras.
This, my generation, we few,
  remember how it was,
  see how it is becoming,
  wonder what it shall be—
  wonder, Lord, not with fear,
  but with expectant anticipation,
  eager to see what you are about.
For you are at work in the world.

I want to participate in your "work in the world."
I want to live my years to the hilt,
  for becoming forty is as exhilarating
  as becoming twenty-two ever was.
  And who knows what new challenge becoming sixty
  or eighty or a hundred
  may hold?
Lord of all my life,

                    amen!

Total commitment, Lord,
   is getting the bills paid on time,
   instead of putting it off just because it is a dull and
      colorless task.
      And it is a priority of stewardship,
         arranging my finances so that my bills are worthy
            bills.

Total commitment
   is getting the kitchen floor mopped when it needs it,
   or leaving it unmopped when my child needs me—
      and having the wisdom to know which is when.

Total commitment?
   Lord, God! It's a phrase that haunts me.
   Total is such an absolute sort of word—
      an all-of-life sort of word—
         with no little private compartments kept back for
            me.
   Commitment is a surrender sort of word—
         a not-my-will-but-thine attitude toward every
            day.

I run. I shudder. I want no part of it.
So *why* does it haunt me so?
Why do you keep it in my mind, ringing in my other ear?
Can't I beg off? Can't we settle for something less?
Must I agonize over all thy needy children?
Must I sacrifice?
My own burdens are enough, Lord. Must I bear these
   others also?

   Total?
      Commitment?
         To thee.

                    Amen.

Lord,
I could have clobbered them all.
They *know* better.
They just don't *do* better.
And I told them so.
You know.
   I told them too much,
            too loud,
            too long.
Still fuming, I turned back to see my Least One,
   making meatloaf,
   squishing the ingredients between her
   I-hope-they-were-clean fists.
In the sudden quiet I could hear her sing,
   "Little hands,
   loving hands,
   busy hands,
      That's me!"
And her smile was a beatitude.

Father, forgive my seething,
   my too-much-ado-about-everything.
   Forgive my pettiness,
   when I work myself into such a stew.
My hands are not small—
   but they needn't be so blundering,
            so clumsy.

They should be busy—
   about matters of consequence.
They should be loving—
   even as they chasten.

Bless her busy, loving little hands.
And bless mine, too.

          Amen.

Thank you, Lord,
    for these other people's children—
        with whom my son plays baseball,
        with whom my daughter shares confidences,
        with whom my small ones play
            and squabble
            and learn that life is composed of relationships.

The things they learn at the hands of their peers
    I could never teach them.
The joys—and the heartaches—
    dished out by their friends
    add color and life to their childhood.
    And—much more.
        Now is their training ground.
        Now is their time of becoming.
        What they become, Lord, is deeply affected
            by these other people's children.

So they, too, become my responsibility.
And—may it be so—my blessing.
They are mine to instruct
                    and chasten
                    and love, while they are at my house.
They are mine to befriend,
and mine to act responsible before.

Bless them, Lord,
and my own.
And me.

                    Amen.

Lord, seems reasonable to expect that
mothers would lose their marbles quicker than other
people.

Like when that wretched boy let his snake get loose—
and lost—in the house.
Like working-on-his-car grease on the carpet—
and the curler that was just the right size to fall down
the bathroom sink.
Like the kids' forgetfulness and thoughtlessness and
rowdiness and everlasting pranks.
Seems reasonable to expect that we mothers should be
the first to go all to pieces.

But, Lord, you seem to have built into us a safety valve.
You seem to have given us a strength, a re-
silience.
I'm stronger *because* of my kids.
And my life is infinitely richer.
Oh, they've added a few gray hairs, true.
But they have also added a depth,
and color, every conceivable shade,
and beauty, and whimsy,
and purpose, and challenge, and fun—
sheer rib-tickling fun—
to the days of my life.
I thank thee, Lord, for this motley crew,
who dare me
and beckon me
and priest to me
and graciously bestow upon me their love.

Amen.

Lord,
I search for some sense in life.
I look for some tomorrow
   when I shall see.
   And know.
And then life shall be so much more meaningful.
But what I've got is today.
   I see dimly.
   I know little.
   and life is very ordinary.
So I wait for tomorrow, dreamily,
   and thumb-twiddle away my today.
Vague anticipation of my own spiritual fulfillment
   someday
   robs me of the *only* day that is truly mine.

Lord, God,
   you have called me to live in the *now*.
Air castles and ambiguities aren't for real.
Life is.
If this were the only day I had on earth,
   what would I do with it?
This *is* the only day I have right now.
   I dare not waste it.

Lord, keep me keenly, sharply aware
   of the immediacy of my living.
   Keep me vitally awake
   this day.

            Amen.

Lord,
it takes two hands to clap.
It takes a total involvement—
        a caught-up-ness—
        to respond to thee.

Clapping is joy
        and response
        and approval
        and saying, "I'm with you.
        Amen!"
And it takes two hands to clap.

One hand behind me, holding back,
   won't do it.

Clapping is enthusiasm.
   (Lord God, I cannot escape thee!
   Enthusiasm—*en theos*—possessed by God!)

     enthusiasm, with a little *e*,
   is a polite and brittle expression
   of a shallow sanction.

Enthusiasm—*possessed* by thee?
   Oh, may it be so!
   May there be no withholdings.

   Lord, possess my life.
   Take these, my hands—
     both of them.

              Amen.

Lord,
  she sees colors I didn't know were there.
Part of it is training, I suppose, because she *is* an artist.
Part of it is *looking*.

The tree trunk I saw was grey;
  she saw it lavender and amber and rose.
  And then, through her eyes, I could, too.
That hillside of trees—a bank of green, I thought.
She saw highlights of absinthe and gold,
  shadows of teal and charcoal and forest green,
  subtle tones and shades and play of light.

So today I look with new eyes on this wondrous world.
I look for all the myriad colors
  and all the tiny detail of design
  in what you have wrought.
What delight you must have taken in fashioning an
  artichoke—
  and a ladybug—
  in putting the colors on a grasshopper's wing
  and in the flamboyant sunset sky.
I look with new eyes on this wondrous world.
I see infinite patience
  and care
  and love.
I see thee.

                    Amen.

Lord,
as I recall, you didn't promise me a bowl of cherries.
You promised a task,
              a yoke,
              a sword.
And these I have.
For in accepting thee,
   I accept an impossible task,
   and an inescapable yoke,
   and the heavy encumbrance of a sword.

But I have the bowl of cherries, too!
   Along with the task comes strength.
   Along with the yoke comes partnership.
   Along with the sword comes challenge
      and a call to adventure.
I find laughter in my mornings—
   and love and joy in all my days.
I *sing* while I mop—
   and pray with thanksgiving as I peel potatoes.
I find rest in my labor,
   deep joy even in my grief.

Lord, my bowl of cherries runneth over!

              Amen.

Dear Lord,
they called it the "Eye of God."
It hung in the gift shop . . .
   just a cross of twigs
   neatly woven through with colored yarn.
   And around it a thousand other irrelevant things.
The eye of God.

My grandfather spoke of the "all-seeing eye of God"—
   and I shivered in my boots
   because it was a malevolent, condemning vision.
But, Lord, that isn't what you are like.
You aren't looking for misdeeds,
   but for moments of splendor,
   newly sprouted shoots of becomingness.
Looking, you see
   my needs
   and my aspirations.
You perceive my hurts
   and my hungers.
You see the struggle that I have
   with my own lesser self.
You see me as I am,
   and you see me as you meant me to be.

And seeing all this,
   you love me anyway.

                O Lord, my God,
                 I kneel in wonder.

        Amen.

Lord, I would open my arms to all of life,
    savoring each contact
    with every other living soul,
    savoring every experience which is part of my life.

Let me no longer hide behind mask or wall,
    for I do not need that sort of protection.
    I walk free in thy world.
Let me relish every moment,
    look with eager anticipation
    toward every new day—
    willing to embrace grief or pain
        as well as joy,
    for all are a part of my completeness.

Let there be no withholding,
                no begrudging,
                no running-and-hiding.
Let me be a participant in living,
    and not merely an onlooker.
Let me be aware,
            awake,
            alive.
Let me savor my depths and heights,
                fears and comforts,
                    unspeakable joys and exquisite pain.
Life is no easy, level plain.
I would not want it so.
    Life is a song to sing
    and a place in the sun!
    Let me *live* it to the hilt!

                    Amen.

Dear Lord,
   you know her.

And she knows you.

Maybe this explains it.
But when she walks into a room,
   people *see* her
   and begin to gravitate toward her.
When she stops by my house,
   something singing happens.
When she talks, it's re-creative,
and when she listens, it's . . . well . . . redemptive.
I know why.
It's the inexplicable magnetism of a person who has
   seen.

Because she has seen,
   she knows where she is going.
   She is in tune with the universe.
   Her real decisions are already made—
      her priorities established.
That being so, the other things fall into place,
   and there is a peace and order about her living.
She has that rare serenity
   that *is* magnetic.
Because she has seen.

Seen what, Lord?
   Seen herself?
   Seen her world?
   Seen thee?

   Ah, so.

           Amen.

Dear Lord,
    what sort of people am I teaching my children to be?
If I criticize them constantly, they will *become* critical.
If I undermine their worth-ness, they will *become* un-
    worthy.
If I am impatient, I teach impatience.
Much of what they will become
    is my doing . . .
    or my undoing.

And I don't think of this, Lord.
I just try to blunder through *today*—
    meeting today's deadlines,
    tending to at least a portion of today's chores.
    I'm not so much raising them
        as just puttering about while they grow up.
And what an irretrievable waste of opportunity *this* is.

Lord, you know what I'd like them to be—
    worthy adults,
    real people
    whose hands will bless, whose words will bless,
    whose lives will bless those around them.

I want them to be the kind of people
who are *at home* in the universe.
Ah, so.
One hand in theirs, Lord,
the other hand in thine—
this is the only way I can lead them.

Amen.

Dear Lord,
    I don't remember the conversation at all—
    just that one sentence
    and the long pause, while we stood there, tasting the
        phrase, mulling over its implications.
    At thirteen, she had not intended to philosophize.
    At thrice that, I had not expected her to.
        But the sentence still hangs there,
        suspended,
        in my consciousness—
"You can't paint by number all your life."

Why, Lord?
    It's so much easier.
    And it makes a prettier picture than I could ever do
    alone.
        I think.
        Except that there is something stilted about it.
        Especially close up.
        I have never been *moved* by a paint-by-number
            picture.

And yet I keep clutching at a paint-by-number life.
I want rules, guidelines,
        neat compartments already labeled,
        decisions predetermined for me.

I have never attempted to create a picture on clean
canvas.
I wonder what would happen if I did.

I wonder what would happen if I launched out on my
very own pattern of living,
        exuberantly—
        relishing the possibilities,
        delighting in the choice of colors,
        blending with finesse,
        mixing wildly,
        shading delicately,
    choosing—free to decide—creating a life-style that
        is mine alone,

and expressing with every honest stroke
   life
      and love
         and thee.

                 Amen.

She wrapped it carefully, Lord,
   tenderly—
      a quarter, a dime,
      a nickel, and a penny.
   She placed them precisely in a rescued soap wrap-
      per, neatly closed its top.
And then, in her very best first-grade printing, she
wrote:

What is in this box is for Love

And then she gave it to her grandmother and grand-
   daddy.

This was an *after*-Christmas gesture,
            an unexpected gift of the heart.

True giving knows no season,
            requires no reason.
            It is for love.

Lord, have I forgotten what it was like to give as a
child gives?
Has my generosity become overlaid
with what the world expects of me,
   with what it costs,
   with what might be appropriate?

Let my giving be spontaneous—
   perhaps unorthodox—
      without season
      or reason,
      or strings attached.

Let it be simple,
   overflowing,
   because I love.
                  Amen.

O Lord,
   I thank you for memories.
   There is comfort
      and soothing balm
      in recollecting past movements of love and joy.

When it is bitterly cold outside,
   it is pleasant to·remember an August wiener roast.
And when the sun is hot,
   and the summer air oppressively still,
   that's when the kids go get the snowballs out of the
      freezer, and we remember the sharp, clean tang of
      a snowy day and the snowboy with the carrot
      nose.

More than this—
Lord, when I am almost overwhelmed with trouble
   or sorrow,
   I remember a cardinal singing in a tree outside the
      window, and my heart is lifted for a moment.
   Without such memories dark moments would be
   almost unbearable.

Thank you for a mind so constructed
   that it has this delightful power of recall—
   so often without my will.
And thank you, too,
   for cardinals, and snowboys, and running through
   fallen leaves,
   and the faces of friends—
for all the wealth of past days
   stored up for me by a mind so constructed,
   to be brought forth when needed and savored
   again.
Thank you, Lord.

                    Amen.

Dear God,
I shall pray again my Least One's New Year's prayer:
"Our Lord!
　　We thank you for this New Year—
　　and all the fun things that's gonna happen!"

May I so regard my new year—
　　　　　　　　my every new day—
　　　　　　　　　anticipating,
　　　　　　　　　　　eager to receive whatever is gonna
　　　　　　　　　　　　happen,
　　　　　　　　　　　eager to participate in what the
　　　　　　　　　　　　days may hold.

Here I come, with both eyes open!
　　Wide awake and *prepared*. . . .
　　　　Well, not really, Lord.
　　　　But if I am going to live on behalf of all mankind,
　　　　　I *need* to be prepared.
　　　　　I need to know who all mankind is
　　　　　　　　　and what all mankind needs.
　　　　　I need to be wide awake.
　　　　　And prepared. And if that means study and
　　　　　　　　　work
　　　　　　　　　and applied thinking,
　　　　　　　　　I'd best have at it.

Because here, before me, is my new year—
　　my new day,
　　with all the fun things
　　and valid things
　　and splendid things that's gonna happen!

Thank you, Lord.

　　　　　　Amen.

Lord,
    we sang it as a hymn when I was a child.
I thought I had outgrown it—
    for its theology is traditionally conservative
    and its terminology old-fashioned.

"Leaning on the everlasting arms. . . ."

Just humming it brings back faces, places—
    people I knew in the church where I grew up.
    I can see them singing it—
    some of them with the fervor of real conviction.

O Lord, my God,
    there are times when today's modern concepts
        and bright phrases, valid though they may be,
        are not enough.
    There are times when what I really need most
        is the deep awareness
        of thy waiting, everlasting arms,
          which are my comfort
          and my refuge
          and my strength.

    In thee do I put my trust,

              Amen.

O Lord, my God,
    In thee do I put my trust,
    for thou art God.
    I remember praying once,
        "Okay, Lord—just come out and let me see you.
        Just let me see for once what you are really like,
        instead of hiding behind your godliness."
And I remember apologizing right quickly,
    just in case there were going to be lightning bolts.

Oh, the audacity of little me,
    that I should want a six-foot God—
        whom I could comprehend
        and understand
        and fathom . . .
        and buddy with!
Oh, the littleness of me.

For thou art *God!*
    The blinding glory of thy face I could not bear.
    The incomprehensible majesty of the Lord of the
    universe . . .
        I stand in awe,
        for thou art God.

And yet, because of a Love, which also I cannot comprehend,
    I see thee, Lord, God,
    reaching out to me—
    making possible a communication.
        I kneel
        before thee—
        for thou art *God.*

Amen.

But, Lord,
   I've always bought brown sugar
      in square boxes
      with brown letters on the box.

I saw the plastic bags of sugar in the grocery store
   yesterday.
I could tell by looking that this was a better way. The
   strong, air-tight bags would keep the sugar soft and
   usable.
But I've *always* bought brown sugar
   in boxes.
   And I reached for the box.

Now, back at home, I wonder why.

Lord, why are we . . .
   why am I . . .
   so reluctant to change old ways?
   Some old ways are valid,
   but some need changing.
And I cling to square boxes with unthinking tenacity,
   just because I've *always* bought square boxes.

That is not reason enough.
Times have changed—and are changing
   so fast it makes my head swim.
I am obligated to face my days intentionally!
   The container that brown sugar comes in is no great
      thing.
   But there are other, weightier matters
      that require rethinking—and perhaps revising.
   If I am going to live significantly,
      I must make my big decisions purposefully,
                                    intentionally,
                                    comprehensively,
"New occasions teach new duties; Time makes ancient
   good uncouth.

They must upward still, and onward, who would keep
abreast of Truth."

Forgive my square boxes.

Amen.

Oh Lord,
   when I wonder whether I am getting anywhere at
   all—
      or why I even try—
let me not forget:

> "A drop in the bucket
> Is only a drop—
> A minor and moist detail;
> For a drop can't change
> The color and taste
> In a ten-quart watering pail.
>
> But if the drop
> Has the color of love
> And the taste of tears divine,
> One drop dropped into
> the vessel of life
> Can turn the water to wine."*

Amen.

* From *For Heaven's Sake* by Helen Kromer © 1961 by Helen Lenore Kromer. Permission for its use must be obtained from Baker's Plays, Boston, Mass.

Oh, that I knew where I might find thee!

Elijah prayed it, Lord.
And Handel prayed it.

So I pray, too.

I have sought thee piously
   in church on Sunday morning
   and have not found thee—
   for my fragmented, daily mind had no room.
I have sought thee frantically,
   when troubles seemed about to overwhelm,
   and have not found thee—
   for what I wanted was Instant God,
   and I had not made time for establishing basic
   relationships.
I have sought thee sporadically in the cloister of the
woods
   and in the clarion color of autumn leaves
   and have not found thee—
   only indications of thy presence there before me.
I have sought thee aimlessly, when things weren't really
   going too well
   and the *hu-mali-mali* of my days seemed rather
   pointless,
   and have not found thee—
   because my seeking was only a vague discontent
   or a self-improvement campaign.

Oh, that I knew where I might find thee!

And the voice of God came to Elijah, saying:
        "If with all your heart you truly seek me,
          you shall ever surely find me."
And the voice of a Galilean carpenter came to those
who were gathered on the hillside, saying,

  "Blessed are those who hunger and thirst for
  righteousness, for they shall be satisfied."

Hunger, Lord? And thirst?
Seek with *all* my heart?
  And I shall ever surely find thee.

                    Amen.

Dear Lord,

he must have been a godly man to have been able to pray so.

> "I am no longer my own, but Thine;
>> Put me to what thou wilt: Rank me with whom Thou wilt;
>> Put me to doing; put me to suffering;
>> Let me be employed for Thee, or laid aside for Thee;
>> Exalted for Thee, or brought low for Thee;
>> Let me be full; let me be empty;
>> Let me have all things: let me have nothing.
>> I freely and heartily yield all things to Thy pleasure and disposal;
>> And now; O Glorious and Blessed God;
>> Father, Son, and Holy Spirit;
>> Thou art mine; and I am Thine
>> And the covenant which I have made on earth be ratified in Heaven."*

Amen.

O Lord,

Amen.

---

* John Wesley.

Dear God,
    whose other name is Love,
it's hard, through tears, to see that you are Love. Right
    now I'm conscious only of the overwhelmingness of
    my grief and the emptiness of today and tomorrow.
And I beat against heaven's doors and say it cannot be
    that this has happened—
        not to us,
        not to me,
        not to mine.
It cannot be that God Almighty, whom I have worshiped
    since my youth, would allow it to happen.
And I know with a detached clarity that it has . . .
    that there is something very final about death,
        something irrevocable,
        that my beating on heaven's doors shall not alter
           that which is.
But even in my anguish there comes a measure of un-
derstanding, of acceptance.
    It's all right, Lord. I know that you love him and
    that you care for him now in his death as you cared
    for him yesterday in his life.
I know that you love us—
    that you understand our lack of understanding—
        that your love will

                sustain us,
                teach us,
                strengthen us,
                and bring us at last, through our
                    love for him, closer to thee—

              if we let it.
Dear God, whose other name is Love.

        Amen.

Dear Lord,
    there just isn't a word for it in English.
    Pope John said it in Italian—
       aggiornamento—
    "the opening up of windows to let in fresh air."
Ah, Lord, I like what it does to a house—
    opening windows.
    The fresh air revives
            and rejuvenates
            and makes me want to sing.
But this *aggiornamento* implies an opening up of windows of the mind—
    an airing out of stale notions and worthless attitudes.
    It implies a reviving and rejuvenating
        that is as welcome as a summer breeze.

I *know* how to open house windows,
    and I do it whenever possible.
I have a fairly good idea how to open windows in my
    mind. But I avoid it whenever possible.
But I *can* deliberately expose my mind to situations
           where study is required,
           where thinking is essential,
           where startling, fresh new ideas are thrust
           upon me.
The crux of the matter is that it takes an act of
    decision to open a window . . .
        in a house
        or in a mind.

Aggiornamento!

                Amen!

Dear Lord,
  forgive us our tranquility.
Ours is a comfortable church.
The pews are foam padded and the carpet soft.
The air conditioning is properly adjusted,
  and the light is soft for the prayers,
    bright for the loud hymns.
Required participation is minimal,
  and *thinking* is almost never required of me.
It's a comfortable church.

Lord, this isn't quite fair.
For there are those within my comfortable church who
  worship honestly, and serve sacrificially.

But so many of us . . . .
  (Ah, Lord, it is for *myself* I pray.)
But *I* am resting on the foam-padded cushions of tran-
quility.
  I *like* air conditioning, but I yearn for significance.

            Set us afire, Lord,
              Stir us, we pray!
            While the world perishes
              We go our way,
            Purposeless, passionless,
              Day after day.
            Set us afire, Lord,
              Stir us, we pray!*

Lord, it is for myself I pray,
but it is also for my church,
  for thy church.
    Set *us* afire.

                    Amen.

* From *I Have a Stewardship* by Ralph S. Cushman. Copyright renewal 1967 by Maud E. Cushman. Used by permission of Abingdon Press.

Lord, I forget.
   I get wrapped up in my own daily affairs
      and don't think about anybody else.
   Like old friends, whom I have not gone by to see for
      so long.
   Like new neighbors,
      for strangers are merely friends I haven't met.
What a travesty!
What a shameful waste!

Friendships have to be intended,
   or they don't happen.

   I wrote, because I hurt for her, and wanted to ease
      for one small moment, her aloneness.
   And, in answering, she wrote between the lines, giv-
      ing me permission to be a part of her life at a
      crucial time.
   For friendship is not only giving,
      but also receiving;
      not only a going to,
      but a being invited in.

There are those I know, casually, whose unique insights
   would enrich my life.
There are those I know, casually, who hunger for friendship,
   whose loneliness is a constant, chilling thing.
   They too have much to give.
Lord, friendships have to be intended,
   and tended.

Bless us all.

                    Amen.

Realizing that I owe Mr. Webster a debt of gratitude for having compiled the dictionary in the first place, I'm a mite affronted at this one:

stupid (adj.) wanting in understanding; obtuse; dull of perception.

Ah, Lord.
That's me.
I never really thought of myself as stupid.

But wanting in understanding? Yes, more's the pity—when my eldest cries out in protest against the hide-bound traditions of the past.
Obtuse? Yes, when my neighbor comes to borrow a cup of sugar, but really needs to borrow strength for her day.
Dull of perception? Ah, so.
Seeing, I perceive not.
My vision checks out 20-20,
but my insight is out of focus.

Stupid?
Yes, it applies.
But it needn't be a permanent state of affairs.
I can *decide* to be otherwise.
I can take time to *listen* to what cannot be said and *see* what cannot be shown
and *perceive* what is beneath the surface.
Forgive my stupidity.
Guide my tomorrows.

Amen.

Lord, I am not alone.
For this I give thanks.
There are times when joy is an uncontainable cup-
running-over—
too delicate to share, too sweeping to bear.
And I am not alone.
There are times when troubles overwhelm—too
nameless to share, too trying to bear.
But I am not alone.
There are times when sorrow engulfs me—
too deeply personal to share, too devastating to
bear.
But I am not alone,
for thou art with me.

Sometimes I forget, and *feel* alone.
You know
how I have ached with appalling loneliness within a
crowd,
or with the unbearable isolation of four walls,
knowing it is not walls which isolate—
panicky, cowering, whimpering inside, and feeling
alone.

The fault was mine, for you were there.
Always have been.
Always will be.

I am not alone.
There is no situation, no circumstance,
no place, no time, no experience
which is apart from thee.
For thou art with me . . .
and within me.

May I remember, always,
that I am not alone.

Amen.

"It is God's will," she said, oozing unctuousness.

Thy will, Lord, that a young mother should die in a
senseless car wreck?

Thy will that a house should burn or a tornado strike?

Thy will that an immortal soul should be begotten in
such a casual and thoughtless way?

O Lord, whose other name is Love, *it is incompatible
with thy nature* to will such as these.

You allow them to happen, Lord—
evil, and disaster, and untimely death.

You have established an orderly universe,
governed by natural laws.
I have not learned all the laws,
nor learned how to live with some I *do* know.

But you do not sit "up there" dispensing misery,
to make me strong—or to try me.
That is incompatible with thy nature.

Tragedy comes—not "sent" by thee, but it comes.

So what *is* thy will in the situation, Lord?

That I should fold my hands in meek acceptance?

No!

It must be thy divine will for me to accept what comes
and grow because of it
and create out of it a new and better situation.

At no other moment in my life will I have so great an
opportunity to become one with thee
as in that moment when all security is snatched away,
and I must cope with Life as its deepest level.
Thy will, thy will be done.

Amen.

Dear Lord,
    There are occasions when you call me to be an
        enabler.
I really like to do the solo parts,
    to be the one who gets the credit for the completed
    task.

        Little me.
        The credit is irrelevant.
        It is the completion of the task that matters.
Sometimes the task calls for someone else to do the
    solo, and I need to play the accompaniment,
        enabling another to take the lead,
            for the sake of the task itself.
Enabling.
That doesn't mean standing aside.
It means *assuming* a supporting role.
It means *seeing* needs, sensing solutions,
    and being willing to risk my personal plaudits for
        the sake of the task.
So . . .
    I will play the part of a whetstone.

                    Amen.

Dear Lord, I haven't time to pray.
The tyrant clock commands my day.

It rousts me out of peaceful bed
In harsh and strident tones I dread.
While breakfast cooks, it watches me,
Marking time relentlessly.
It urges me to hurry on
Until the kids are ready, gone.
But nagging still, it goads me more
To wash the dishes, sweep the floor,
Get myself all dressed to go
To scheduled meetings in a row.

Never letting up a tick!
Lord, I haven't time to pray.
The tyrant clock commands my day.

That's not true, is it, Lord?
The clock is no tyrant. It's merely a box of gears, invented to measure time.
I must command my day—
and all my days.
The clock is an aid by which I can gauge my plans,
by which I can organize my tasks.
The choice of tasks is mine.
I must command my day—

Lord, I need thy guidance.
My plans must be worthy ones,
worked out in a set-apart time with thee.

Amen.

Dear Lord,
  I have been waiting,
    knowing how much she hungered to talk,
    making myself available to her,
    standing by.
  And the long days pass,
    and the weeks,
    and still she hungers to talk.
  I can see it in her eyes.
  I can hear it in the bright, brittle way she skirts
    around what is uppermost in her mind.
Dear Lord,
  guide me,
  lest I trespass upon the private soul of another.
  But I must barge in,
  for her sake,
  and help her say what she wants to have said,
  help her face what she must face—
    openly,
    frankly.
I must barge in
  with love,
  so that the things we shall say will be said in the
    presence of Love.
  I may not understand,
  but I can give her the strength and support of my
  concern.
  And I can give her the blessed release of having put
    her problem into words.
Dear Lord,
  help me barge in gently.

                    Amen.

Bless my mother, Lord.

She dragged all those heavy logs and brush up to the house and bought wieners and marshmallows—"just in case" we might come up that evening with the kids.

Bologna sandwiches would have been much simpler. I told her so.

"But the children wouldn't remember eating just bologna sandwiches," she said. "They will remember a wiener roast."

And they did. They do.

Stored up along with all the other choice bits to remember.

Some of those memories "just happened."

But a goodly number of them she *caused* to happen.

She has a way of deliberately setting into motion an Occasion . . .

> which becomes a memory to cherish.

Bless my mother, Lord!

And let me learn this, too, from her—
this knack of *creating* memories.
I can do it for my own family,
setting in motion
a memorable moment,
adding the flair
that makes it an Occasion.

I can do it for others, too.
It's a matter of caring.
It's a matter of loving—
not off-handedly
but deliberately, *care*-fully, *thought*-fully.

Let me learn this, too, from her.

Amen.

Dear Lord,
    Everybody knows the monsters can't get you
      if you just stay under the covers.
I remember, from childhood, sticking one toe out of
my bed—
    sure that Something out there would *grab* it—
    and it was a delicious exercise in agony,
    a shivering ghost-story fear,
      for I knew I was safe
      under the covers—
    the familiar, enclosing covers
      and my own solid, dependable bed.
Now I stick out one toe—
    talking wisely about the monsters of the day,
    shivering in my exercise of fear,
    knowing that I'm safe
    as long as I stay under the covers . . .

Under the covers of the familiar, hugging close to me
    the status quo;
under the covers of ignorance, hiding behind
      not knowing-what's-going-on-out-there;
under the covers of preoccupation,
    too busy with my own affairs to pay more than fleeting
    attention to the monsters.
But the monsters today are real,
    and my covers are no protection.

Lord, today is different from yesterday—
    vastly and horribly and wonderfully different!
    And I've got to face it,
    status quo thrown off like a discarded quilt.
    Ignorance is no defense,
    preoccupation no excuse.

Lord, forgive my ostrich-headed, cover-clinging past.
Wake me up to what's going on in the world.
Let me throw off the covers and jump out of bed—
    right into the midst of things—
    seeing that they aren't *monsters*
      but monstrous possibilities

that must be faced, seized by the foretop,
and used for building today's world
according to thy divine blueprint.

Amen.

Lord, I got out of the *same* side of the bed that I always get out of . . .
so what went wrong?
I stumped my toe on the doorjamb.
The toast burned.
The big kids were crabby.
And then I discovered that my Least One had bro-
ken out with the *chicken pox*—
this being the week I had planned to sew
and paint the kitchen.

My Pollyanna friend would probably say everything
would turn out just fine.
Nuts!
Come to think of it, Lord, she's the sort who would set
about *making* it turn out just fine.
She could undoubtedly see opportunities in the situation which escape me—
when I'm already miffed, and my toe hurts.
She'd accept what the situation *is, now,*
and then make the absolute most of it!

Chicken pox? What a delightful opportunity to have
one child at home *alone*—
to bake cookies with,
to make models with, and read stories to.
What a delightful opportunity to store up memories of good times together!

Lord, I need to devote myself to *making* things turn
out fine.
I need the insight to *see* possibilities in the situation
as it is,
and then the gumption to *do.*
Thank you, God, for chicken pox.

Amen.

Lord, I *like* that new song!

> I cannot come—don't trouble me now.
> I have married a wife,
> I have bought me a cow.
> I have deals and commitments
>   that cost a pretty sum.
> Pray hold me excused . . .
>   I cannot come.*

The music is so positive and contemporary,
    and the words are so. . . .

> Good grief, Lord!
> The words are so dreadfully incriminating!

I cannot teach a Sunday school class—
    don't trouble me now.
> Taking the time to prepare a *valid* lesson deprives
> my family of attention I should be giving them.
>   I cannot come.

I cannot go to the precinct meeting—
    don't trouble me now.
> I have no training in politics,
> and I simply must get some sewing done.
>   Pray hold me excused. . . . I cannot come.

O Lord, my God,
    how tired you must get of my excuses!
You call me—over and over—
    in ways I am too "stupid" to recognize—
and you call me in ways that I recognize perfectly well.
And I, preoccupied with my own deals and commit-
    ments, ask to be excused. I cannot come.
God, forgive.

Amen.

* Granted by permission of Vanguard Music Corporation, 240 West
57th St., New York, N. Y. 10019, from the record *Joy Is Like the Rain*,
Avant Garde Records, 250 W. 57th St., New York, N. Y.

Dear Lord,
    I found a word—a new, free-flying sort of word—
        cadenza: "that portion of a concerto where the
        soloist is permitted to build some fanciful improvi-
        sations upon the straight musical facts which con-
        front him."
    How like you, God,
    to set up life like that—
    with room for cadenzas!
There is a musical score,
    and, if my living is going to be in harmony,
        I need to follow that score.
But then, there is
                a place for—
                a *need* for—
                        cadenzas.

I'm different.
My parts—solo or background—add to the beauty of
    my total orchestration.
And my cadenzas are unique—
    my own *personal* contribution.
Cadenzas arise out of a confidence—a sureness—
    and out of a lilting need to sing.

Lord, take from me my fears, my unsureness,
    my reluctance to play *my own* composition,
        with its light and airy grace notes
        and its basso profundo of faith.
Let me play my cadenzas,
    unfettered by the "rules" of the score,
    with that freedom born of knowing and abiding by
    the rules.

The world is thine, and I am thine.
    What should I fear?

            Amen.

Lord,
    I'm really never sure what I would do in a given sit-
    uation.

I don't *think* I'm a hit-and-run driver.
But I've never actually been in that situation,
    so how can I be sure?
I don't *think* I could ever steal.
    But my children have never been hungry,
    so how can I be sure?

It is easy for me to pass judgment on others,
    but sometimes I wonder what I'd do
        in their circumstances.
I have known fear—and panic.
    I don't always think rationally in the presence of
        fear. . . . I don't always *think*.
What would I be like, backed into a corner—
    with my security wrenched from me?

Lord, I wonder sometimes what I'm *really* like—
    under the veneers.

If my security in thee is really firm,
    then it reaches to the inner core,
    and I can accept myself—
        all of me—
        without misgiving.
    I can accept responsibility
        for myself—
        for what I am—
        for whatever I may do—

        for I am thine.

           Amen.

Dear Lord,
the implications are unavoidable.

The morning went so smoothly.
Socks were sorted and put away, so *that* particular crisis never occurred.
The boys had ironed shirts ready,
    and the girls had a choice of freshly starched and mended dresses.
Tempers were mellow. I heard one of them singing as she made her bed, another whistling as he fed the dog, and I realized I was humming myself.

The implications are unavoidable.
Part of my calling
    is a real obligation to attend to daily things—
    to keep the house in reasonable order,
    to prepare the meals on time,
    to keep the washing and ironing sufficiently caught up so that it doesn't plague me or them,
    to establish and maintain an atmosphere that is conducive to relaxed home living.

Such an atmosphere enables all of us—
    husband, wife, child—
        to go out into the world with a head start.
There will be sufficient crises later on in the day.

Part of my calling
    is to attend to daily things.

So be it, Lord.

Amen.

Baba wedu,
muri kudenga—
  she knelt in a grass-roofed church to pray.
Our Father,
who art in heaven—
  I kneel here, Lord, knee-bowed and body-bent before
  thee.

Our Father,
  hers and mine,
  who understands the prayers addressed to thee in all
    the languages of the world—
Our Father,
  whose children are, by their very dependence on
    thee, brothers to each other—
Our *Father,*
  whose love plans for us,
                yearns for our response,
                watches over us—
My Father, who watches over me—
  I kneel
    and worship
      and love.

Amen.

Lord,
　　this is the day I'll knock out the wall.
　　It's been in the way for goodness knows how long—
　　　　an eyesore and an inconvenience.
　　I have known it needed to go,
　　　　but I've put off doing anything about it—
　　　　partly because it's going to be a headache and a
　　　　mess,
　　　　partly because of voluntary inertia.
But this is the day.
I have decided.
　　I will take the necessary measurements
　　　　and then pick up the crowbar
　　　　and knock out the wall.
Ah, so,
　　Lord, there are walls within my mind that surely do
　　　　get in the way.
　　I stumble into them;
　　　　they are an eyesore;
　　　　　　they block my vision;
　　　　　　　　and they shut me off from what I ought to
　　　　　　　　become.
I have known this for some while,
　　but I put off doing anything about it.
　　It takes an act of volition.
　　It takes a deliberate decision
　　　　to knock out a wall.
But *this* is the day.
Thank you, God—
　　　　　　　　and hand me the crowbar!

　　　　　　Amen.

Lord,
  I woke up in a superworld!
  We ate superflakes for breakfast.
  The kids went out to play with a superball
    that bounces three times as high as balls used to
    bounce.
  Then they came in to watch the Saturday morning
    cartoons—
    Super Ghost and Wonder Boy,
    to be followed, right after the spine-tingling
    commercial, by Mighty Monster.
  Nothing's life-size anymore. Nothing's ordinary.
    I can't even buy a box of plain old soap.
    It comes giant-sized, superactivated with power
    granules.

Nothing's ordinary anymore?
Maybe everything's ordinary, Lord.
Maybe life, without thee, is so dull and ordinary that
  it has to be souped up,
    overadvertised with Madison Avenue flourish,
      to make it count at all.
How phony!
How shallow and make-believe.

There isn't a great deal I can do about the nationwide
  overall problem.
But I ought to live so that my children will *catch* some
  of the tingling excitement
    of living *for real*,
    of living *deliberately*,
      in a world that is thine—
        that, because it is thine,
        is fraught with unbelievable possibilities,
        indescribable adventure . . .
        for those who dare!

            Amen.

Dear Lord,
I come confessing.
There are times when I talk too much.
There are times when I repeat things which I have no
  right to repeat.
> I pass on a story which may not be entirely true or
> add my own embroidered flourish to a tale in the
> telling.
Father, forgive.
This is a sin of commission—
  and a dreadful betrayal of confidence.
Forgive,
  and help me remember to keep a deliberate and
  constant check on my tongue.
  Keep safe within me the hurts and secrets that others
    have shared,
      for they are a trust.
  Keep safe within me the confidences of my child,
    lest she be hurt by my crass joking over her tender
    moments.
  Keep safe within me those communications
    which were entrusted to me for safekeeping.

Amen.

Lord,
    how loath am I to *plan* my life.
    If I drew a time line . . .

├───────┼───────┼───────┼──────────────────────┤

    and put in the year of my birth
    and my graduation
    and my marriage
    and the birth years of my children
        and today . . .
    then what would I put?

Well, the end of the line is my death.
    Must I put in a date there, too, Lord?
    (I don't want to. It's hard.)
        To make it graphic, I must enter a year for my
        death.
        Between Now and Then is all I have.
(I don't want to plan it. That's harder still.)
But if I don't plan it, I may just float through it,
    signifying nothing.
    It was not for floating that you gave me the years
    of my life.
Plans can be changed.
    My arms must be open to opportunities that I have
      not even dreamed of.

Plans will of necessity be incomplete,
But plans I must make,
    or my present is indecisive
    and my future vague.
So, Lord, here in thy presence,
    I make a time line,
        entering those milestones of my past . . .
        and today . . .
        and the milestones I can anticipate,
        planning to accomplish these specific things,

planning to grow in these specific ways,
planning to change history where I touch life.

Amen, amen.

Dear Lord,
>   deliver us from *fuss* on Sunday morning!
> I want it to be a good day—
>   pleasant, and meaningful.
>   Thy day—and holy because it *is* thy day.
>   But our dither makes it a day to dread,
>   an *un*-holy mess,
>   unpleasant and meaningless.

My conscience hurts.
I have a feeling that *I* am the monkey wrench in the
>   gears.
Much of the dither is because I don't care enough—
>   don't *really* feel it's important enough
>   to justify my extra efforts.

But if I started on Thursday,
>   getting things ready for Sunday—
>   shirts ironed, mending done,
>   a special Sunday breakfast treat already baked,
>   plans made for a simple noon meal
>   of canned salmon and good pickles or sand-
>   wiches, something that needs not require my
>   sweat or the kids' long wait—
>   if I planned ahead,
>   it could be a perfectly joyous day
>   with time for each other
>   and time for thee.

Who knows but what we might *sing* on the way to
church.
We might have a moment to remind ourselves of the
endless line of splendor that is the historical church.
We might have time to remember what it is to be part
of the Christian community.
We might be in a frame of mind for worship.
Perhaps, if I looked forward—anticipating—

107

to Sunday morning,
my family might also.
Ah, so.

Amen.

She came in storming, "It isn't fair!"
    And it wasn't.
But, Lord, who ever said things were going to be fair?

    Big kids bully,
    and little kids pester,
    and parents deal unjustly,
    and even teachers are, on occasion, blind.

    There are times when her woes are her own doing,
        but there are also times when she is innocent,
            and has been "done to,"
            and it isn't fair.

Help me help her over these rough spots,
    that she may rise above her injustices,
        without bitterness
        or the self-inflicted pain of martyrdom.
She will know other injustices, when it isn't fair.
She can seize them, purposefully—
    rectifying where possible
    or profiting from the buffet.
For the confronting of an unfairness has within it the
    possibility of making her strong and tall
    or weak and small.
Lending her my rose-colored glasses will not help her.
My willingness to see life honestly—
    and trust it anyway—
    is a more valid assist.

I pray for her, Lord.
I pray for me.

                Amen.

Dear Lord,
   my faith contains such splendid, glowing nouns:
      holiness
      benediction
      peace
      heaven.
They are words rich in meaning, and just saying them over brings an image of dimly lighted sanctuaries and stained-glass windows. And I bask in this feeling of goodwill.

But somehow the verbs don't give the same comfortable warmth:

come	forgive
go	work
do	pardon
be	understand
help	love.
console	

They *require* of me.
   They require not just a feeling, but an action.

They require involvement
      and straining my mind
      and getting my hands dirty.
They require more than the self-fulfillment, the receiving of the nouns.
They require an *expenditure* of self for the good of all mankind.
They require of me.
You require of me.
I go.

                    Amen.

110

Our Father, who art in heaven,
   hallowed be thy name.
   I come this day
      aware of thy divine majesty
      and of my humanness.

   I shall always be an apprentice at prayer.
   I can never really *know* thee.
   I can never really *find* thee.
   But my *seeking* is the most valid part of my life.
      I find no rest, except in thee.
While I shall never know thee fully,
   my joy is in the search.
There is a hunger that you have placed within me,
   a need, a restlessness.

Blessed are those who hunger and thirst after
   righteousness.

O Lord, my God,
   I know the hunger.
   I know the thirst.
      And I am blessed.

          Amen, amen.

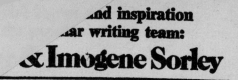